Little Princess Rani and the Palace Adventures

Rani Saves Diwali

By Anita Badhwar

For Vikram and Divya

Thank you to Mom, Dad, Anil
and Peter Gordon
for your support

ISBN-13: 978-1491216033

Rani is a little Princess of a Kingdom in India. Rani has

a pet parrot named Hari.

One morning, Hari carefully sneaked out of his bird cage. He flew over to Rani's bed. Hari saw that Rani was still asleep. "*Namaste! Namaste!*" (Greetings) squawked Hari, but Rani did not wake up. Just as Hari thought about pulling off Rani's blanket to wake her up, Rani woke up.

As she awoke, she saw Hari standing on her bed. "Hari, did you sneak out of your bird cage again?" asked Rani. "I did! I did!" squawked Hari.

Rani laughed. Hari was always up to some tricks.

Rani jumped out of bed because she remembered something special about today. She ran to look at her calendar. It was October 23rd. "Hari, today is *Diwali*, the festival of lights! I can't wait for the celebration this evening!" Rani exclaimed.

"Diwali? Diwali? What's that? What's that?" squawked Hari. Hari had never celebrated Diwali before. "Since this is your first Diwali, Hari, it will be very special," said Rani.

"Diwali is the Hindu festival of lights. It is celebrated around the world as part of the Hindu New Year," continued Rani. "The best part of Diwali is that we get to eat lots of YUMMY *mithai* (sweets) and give out gifts to our citizens!" said Rani.

"In the evening, after Diwali *puja* (prayer), all the *diyas* (clay lamps) will be lit and our family will exchange gifts. It's going to be a lot of fun!" exclaimed Rani. "Lots of fun! Lots of fun!" squawked Hari.

As Rani finished explaining Diwali to Hari, Rani's lady-in-waiting, Jaya, rushed in through the bedroom door.

"Princess Rani, the Maharani has asked to see you immediately," Jaya said.

Rani left right away to see her mother.

"I'm afraid I have some bad news, Rani. Our Royal Decorator has had an accident. He will not be able to finish arranging the diyas or the palace's Diwali lights for the celebration tonight," said the Maharani. "OH NO!" exclaimed Rani.

Rani was worried because she knew that a brightly lit home on Diwali night invites blessings from *Laxmi*, the Goddess of Wealth, for the New Year. It would be unlucky to celebrate Diwali without diyas or lights. Then Rani had an idea.

"Mom, can I finish the decorations?" she asked. "Rani, this is a very big job. Do you think you can do it?" her mother asked. "Sure I can, Mom! I have a plan," said Rani. After they spoke for a few more minutes, her mother agreed to Rani's plan.

Rani returned to her royal bedroom to tell Jaya and Hari the news. "The Royal Decorator has had an accident and cannot finish the decorations," said Rani. "Oh no! Oh no! squawked Hari. "So I asked the Maharani if I could finish the Diwali decorations," said Rani.

"Princess Rani, will you be able to finish ALL the decorations on time?" asked Jaya. "Sure, I can, with your help. We can do it together!" replied Rani. Then Rani asked Jaya to make a list of things that needed to be finished.

"Hari can put up the Diwali lights by flying high up to the palace's rooftops,"
said Rani. "Next, you and I can arrange the diyas. After arranging the diyas,

I need to meet with the Royal Chef to decide on the mithai to give to our
citizens,"said Rani. "Don't forget, we also need to give out the gifts of gold
coins too!" added Rani. "The last thing we need to do is to make *rangoli*

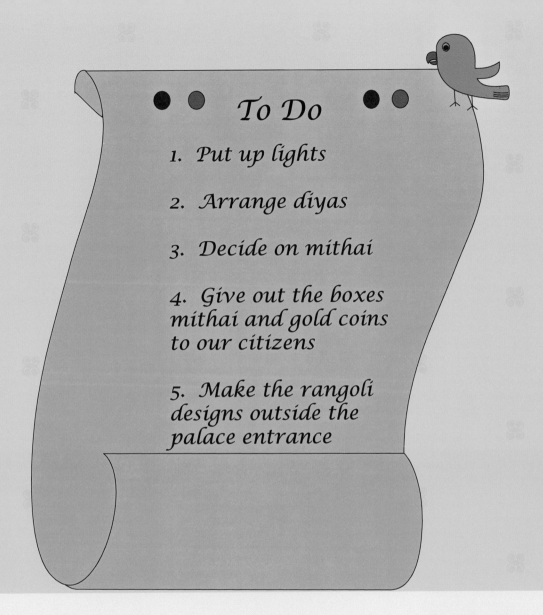

To Do

1. Put up lights

2. Arrange diyas

3. Decide on mithai

4. Give out the boxes mithai and gold coins to our citizens

5. Make the rangoli designs outside the palace entrance

(colored rice powder) designs outside the palace's entrance," said Rani. "Jaya, because you are so talented at making beautiful rangoli designs, you are the perfect person for this job," said Rani.

Rani, Hari and Jaya got to work. Outside the palace, Rani watched as Hari hung up each strand of lights. "All done! All done!" squawked Hari, as he sipped water from the fountain.

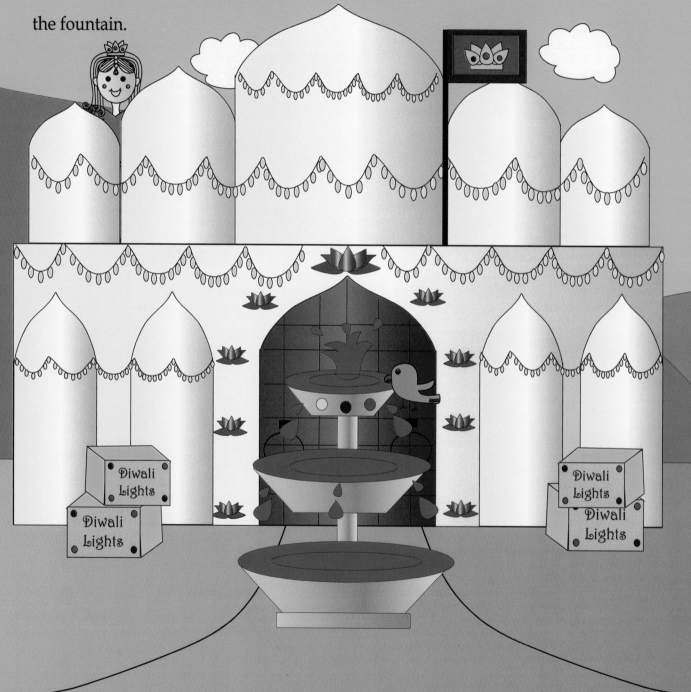

Next, Rani and Jaya arranged the diyas throughout the palace. "Whew!

We are done!" Rani said.

As Rani left to meet with the Royal Chef, Jaya began to put away the boxes.

After tasting different mithai, Rani finally made her selections. "I think we should have an assortment of *gulab jamen*, *jalebi* and *laddoos*," said Rani.

"Excellent choices, Princess! I'll get the boxes ready and pack some extra for you to munch on," said the Royal Chef. "Oh YUMMY! Thank you!" said Rani happily.

After the boxes of mithai were packed, Rani, Jaya, and Hari were ready to leave the palace. They climbed on top of her royal elephant, Bindi. Rani and Jaya were seated inside the royal *palkhi* (palanquin). Hari rode on top.

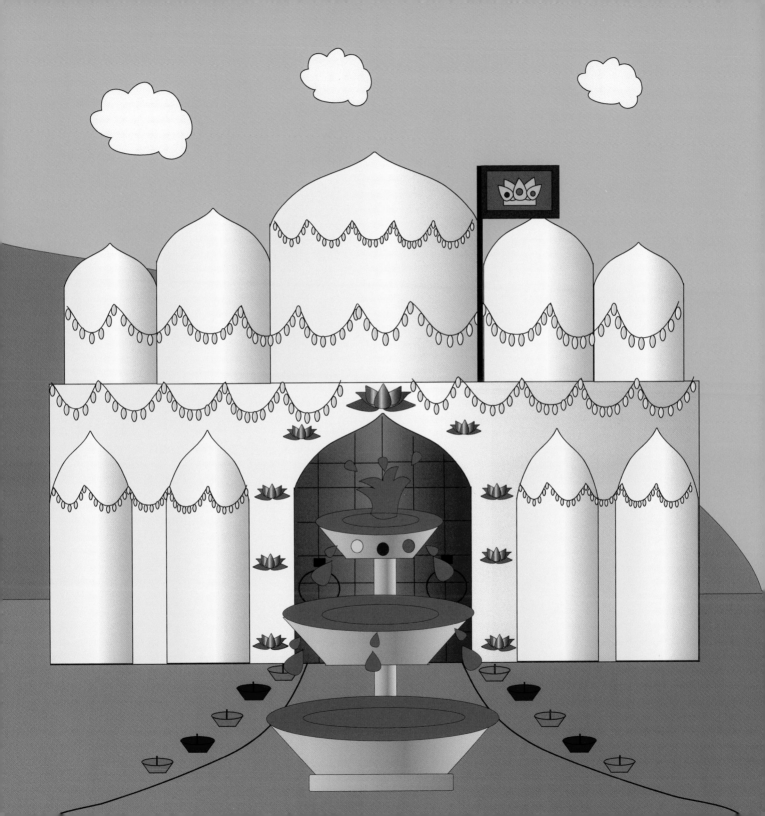

As Bindi walked through the kingdom, Rani and Hari gave out the gold coins. Jaya gave out the boxes of mithai. The citizens waved and cheered. Ladies were dressed in brightly colored *sarees* (wrapped dress) and decorated their hair with jasmine flowers.

Some ladies had their hands painted with *mehndi* (henna). Gentlemen wore *sherwanis* (fancy top and pants). Rani loved the festivities and the beautiful Diwali colors. She also loved eating the yummy mithai!

They returned to the palace just as the sun was setting. Jaya found the rangoli powder and began making the designs on the palace's front walkway. "Beautiful! Beautiful!" squawked Hari. Rani left to meet her mother in the *mandir* (temple).

"Mom, I have good news! Hari put up the lights and Jaya and I arranged the

diyas. After that we still had time to give out the Diwali gifts to our citizens,"

said Rani excitedly. "Once Jaya finishes the rangoli designs, all the Diwali

decorations will be completed," ended Rani. "Oh Rani, that is good news! You

were able to get everyone to work together to save Diwali for us! I can also tell that you enjoyed the mithai, Rani, because your hands are all sticky," said her mother, laughing. Rani and her mother then joined her father, the *Maharaja* (Great King) and her brother, Raja, to begin the puja.

Rani handed a *thali* (tray) to her mother. The thali had puja offerings of milk,

gold, coins, rice, flowers, a diya, mithai and *kum-kum* (red powder).

Rani's family prayed to Lord *Ganesh* (remover of obstacles), Goddess *Laxmi*, and Lord *Kubera*, the God of Wealth. The family prayed for health, wealth, and happiness for themselves, their citizens, and their kingdom.

Once the puja was finished, all the palace's lights were turned on and the diyas

were lit. The diyas and lights made the palace sparkle. Rani and her family

had dinner, and afterwards, exchanged gifts.

Rani even gave Hari a *mala* (necklace) made of gold, as a Diwali present.

"Thank you! Thank you!" he squawked. After saying good night to her family,

Rani and Hari went to her royal bedroom to watch the fireworks.

Rani was so relieved that they were able to finish the Diwali decorations in time for the celebration. Also, she was happy because she knew that Goddess Laxmi would bless them with good fortune for the New Year!

"Did you enjoy the Diwali celebration today?" asked Rani. "I did! I did!"

replied Hari. "Happy Diwali, Hari!" said Rani. "Happy Diwali! Happy

Diwali!"squawked Hari.

After Rani and Hari watched the fireworks, Rani slowly climbed into bed. She did not want the day to end. Rani fell quietly to sleep, with a smile on her face, dreaming about the delicious mithai she ate all day long!

The Meaning of Diwali

Diwali, the Hindu festival of lights, originated in India and is celebrated all over the world. The festival takes place once a year, either in the month of October or November. The festival marks the start of the Hindu New Year.

The festival of Diwali is based on the story of the Hindu God and King, *Ram*, and his wife *Sita*. In this story, an evil King named *Ravana* kidnaps Sita, but Ram rescues Sita after defeating Ravana in an epic battle. When Ram and Sita returned to their Kingdom of *Ayodhya* his citizens celebrated by lighting *diyas* (clay lamps) in his honor. Thus the festival of Diwali symbolizes the triumph of good over evil because Ram defeated the evil Ravana.

On Diwali, *Laxmi puja* (prayer) is performed in the evening. Goddess Laxmi is worshipped because it is believed that she brings good fortune during the coming year to those who pray to her. People will begin this day by cleaning their homes and preparing for evening puja. People will prepare a puja *thali* (tray) which contains milk, money, rice, flowers, a diya, *mithai* (sweets) and *kum-kum* (red powder). These items are used as offerings during puja. Along with worshipping Goddess Laxmi, Lord *Ganesh* is also worshipped on Diwali because it is believed that he removes obstacles prior to the start of any new undertaking. In addition, people also pray to Lord *Kubera* for financial success in the New Year.

As part of the Diwali preparations, people may decorate their porch or walkway with *rangoli* (colored rice powder) which is used to make colorful designs or images of different Hindu gods. People also decorate their homes with lights and arrange diyas which are lit in the evening. It is believed that decorating the house with lights and lighting diyas invites blessings of good fortune from Goddess Laxmi on Diwali night.

Once puja is completed, diyas are lit, and people enjoy an elaborate dinner. People exchange gifts, eat mithai and watch fireworks to end the festivities for the day!

CPSIA information can be obtained
at www.ICGtesting.com
Printed in the USA
LVIC06n1947160714
394636LV00008B/156

* 9 7 8 1 4 9 1 2 1 6 0 3 3 *